TI

SUN TEMPLE

VIKAS A

XpressPublishing
An imprint of Notion Press

XpressPublishing
An imprint of Notion Press

Old No. 38, New No. 6
McNichols Road, Chetpet
Chennai - 600 031

First Published by Notion Press 2019

ISBN 978-1-64760-979-5

Contents

CHAPTER ONE

LOCATION & ACCESSIBILITY

Let me tell you how you can reach Konark. The Konark Sun Temple is located on the Bay of Bengal coastline in the Indian state of Odisha. Konark, the seat of World famous Sun Temple, forms one of the three points of the "Golden Triangle of Tourism" in the State of Odisha, the other two being Bhubaneswar, the city of Temples and Puri, the abode of Lord Jagannath. It is approximately 60 kilometers southeast of Bhubaneswar. The nearest airport is at Bhubaneswar. Trains from various cities of India connect here as well. For travelers flying from Europe or America, the best way to reach Konark is to fly either to Kolkata, Mumbai or Delhi and then fly to Bhubaneswar. Travelers flying from Australia or California could fly directly to Chennai or Kolkata and then fly to Bhubaneswar. The seat of Lord Jagannath, Puri is at a manageable distance of approximately 35 kilometers from Konark. You can get a taxi, bus or local transport very easily at Puri or Bhubaneswar to reach Konark. If you are driving from Puri, it will be your most wonderful ride on road running alongside the continuous stretch of the Bay of Bengal. Also, you can halt alongside to have a taste of local pani puri and refreshing coconut water. On the way from Puri, you will also come across a small village of Pipli with many shops selling a wide collection of handicrafts. If you have time and flexibility, you can halt and buy some of these products. Please make a note that there is also a big market outside the Sun temple where you can buy handicrafts made by local people. The street vendors engulf the entire entrance on both sides, though they have very creative and interesting objects and you can bargain as well. So, carry food for toddlers in case they get hungry during the temple visit. It may interest you to know that the local language of the region is Odia. People here can speak Hindi and English too.

If you plan to stay in Konark for a full-day it is advisable to spend time visiting nearby destination spots that are otherwise abandoned. If traveling by the OTDC or private tour operators - these destinations are either narrated by the bus operators or halted for approximately an hour during the trip. Taxis are always available for local transport in and around Konark, but you will also find Auto Rickshaws. If you want to hire a taxi then ask for the quotation to various travel agents as the rates often vary. Please negotiate the rates before commencing your journey.

Purchase the tickets before entering the compound of the temple. It is about Rs 25 for Indians per head, Handy cam Rs 25 and Rs 600 for international tourists. The entry is free for children below the age of 12 yrs. The ticket rates are subject to change.

After purchasing the tickets walk towards the **Nata Mandira**or **the Dance hall**. While walking you can observe the serene atmosphere coupled with a quiet but majestic sea-shore nearby. When viewed from inland during the dawn and sunrise, the chariot-shaped temple appears to emerge from the depths of the blue sea carrying the sun god. The Chandrabhaga beach is located approximately 3 kilometers from here. It is said that the waves use to reach almost up to the base of the temple during the ancient era and that the sea retreated just over a century ago. The Chandrabhaga beach is considered to be one of the biggest assets of the state as far as tourism is concerned. It is one of the finest, cleanest and greenest beaches in eastern Indiaand is one of the ideal places for holidays.

The Konark Sun temple was declared a World Heritage Site in 1984. The unfathomable intricacy of the carvings at the Temple is unparalleled anywhere in the world. The temple is known for its **Chariot shape, stone-carved wheels,**pillars and the intricate carvings done on the walls. Great poet **RabindranathTagore**once wrote of Konark: "***here the language of stone surpasses the language of man***." It is absolutely true since the experience here cannot be described in words. Please take a look at the green lawns which are well maintained and try to get a glimpse of the white and beautiful cranes flying, which is a rare sight indeed. In the evenings, the Konark temple is lit up with lights that look mesmerizing.

CHAPTER TWO

NATA MANDIRA

The **Nata Mandira**or **the Dance Hall**stands on a high, intricately carved platform. This structure has somehow survived to the current date. However, the roof of this structure no longer exists. This is where the temple dancers used to perform dances in homage to the Sun god. The relief on the platform is similar in style to that found on the surviving walls of the temple. The **NataMandira**is exquisitely carved all across the base up to the top with the images of dancers, flora, hunters, musicians, human life cycle, gods and goddesses and many more. One can take a close look at the sculptures here along with the kids. However, for the principal monument, parental guidance is recommended.

You can see from here, that the alignment of the Sun Temple is in the east-west direction. This **Nata Mandira**is on the eastern side, facing the sea. It is guarded by two huge lions each trying to kill an elephant and each elephant trampling a man below. While the lions represent pride, elephants represent wealth. This depicts a message to humankind that pride and wealth can lead to the downfall of a man. These sculptures are installed on two high stone-benches on either side of the passage to the pillared platform of **Nata Mandira**. You can take the flight of steps to reach the platform of the **Nata Mandira**above and take a quick view of the temple complex too.

The name Konark derives from the combination of the Sanskrit words Kona and Arka. 'Kona' means 'Corner' and 'Arka' means 'Sun'. Therefore Konark is also known as Arka kshetra. The context of the term Kona is unclear. It probably refers to the southeast location of this temple either within a larger temple complex or in relation to other sun temples on the Indian peninsula.

The Konark Temple is dedicated to the Sun God who is popularly known as Surya in India. Surya has been a popular deity since the Vedic period and is regarded as the prime source of life-giving energy and the healer of diseases by Indians. In this context, it is worth noting that Sunlight is essential for the synthesis of Vitamin D and melanin. Also, Surya Namaskar is an important part of yogic practice.

The visible pyramidal structure of Konark Sun Temple which one can see from this dance hall is locally known as **Jagamohana**and is about 128 feet or 39 meters tall. Can you see how magnificent it is? It is just so gigantic so also the stories associated with it are many. **Jagamohana**is thought to have served as a prayer and offering hall for worshipers. The main temple structure or vimana or the sanctum sanctorum was much higher than **Jagamohana**. It was about 229 feet high and was locally known as **DEULA**. It has collapsed and only the ruined walls of the same are standing. Thus, all that you can see as the principal structure is just half of the main temple complex, and even that is damaged. The **DEULA**and the **Jagamohana**differed in size, decorative themes, and design.

The reason as to why this amazing structure was built is a mystery. There is no evidence-based information in this regard. Some say that it was built as a monument of triumph against Muslim invaders. It is also widely believed that this very site has been a place of worship long before the Konark temple was constructed.

A popular legend states that Lord Krishna cursed his son Samba with leprosy. Samba underwent severe penance for **12 years**at Mitravana near the confluence of Chandrabhaga River with the sea at Konark and ultimately succeeded in pleasing the God Surya, who healed Samba of his illness. In gratitude, he erected a temple in the honor of Surya. Since then, this place has been regarded as sacred. Yet, according to another puranic legend Lord Vishnu placed his belongings at several places to commemorate his victory after killing the demon Gyasur. He placed his conch at

Puri, Disc in Bhubaneshwar, Mace in Jajapur and the Lotus at Konark. In Sanskrit, Lotus means Padma and Kshetra means religious zone. Therefore, Konark is also known as Padma-kshetra.

To first get an idea of the enormity of the task of building such a huge structure, let us first circumnavigate the **Jagamohana**and the ruins of the **DEULA** by moving around the outer wall. Do keep attention to find three enormous 11 feet tall Sun god statues which could be seen standing at the tree outside corners of the **Jagamohana**depicting the Sun god at various stages of his journey during a day. Youthful in the morning, at full strength around midday and tired but satisfied at sunset. While you walk towards the collapsed structure of the **DEULA**, let us share some details about its history and collapse.

The main temple is thought to have survived until the time of **Akbar**, the great Indian king because, **Abul Fazl**, the court biographer of Akbar mentions in '**Ain-i-Akbari**' that the temple is in a proper state. He writes: "Near Jagannath (Puri) is a temple dedicated to the sun. Its cost was defrayed by twelve years' revenue of the province. Even those, whose judgment is critical, stand astonished at the sight. 28 temples stand in its vicinity; six before the entrance and 22 within the enclosure, each of which has its separate legend." James Fergusson who visited the temple in **1837**, recorded a corner of the **DEULA**still standing.

The Sun temple was referred to as **'The Black Pagoda'** by the European sailors probably because the top of the temple might have turned black due to weather conditions. It was distinctive from the "**White Pagoda**" – the Jagannath Temple further up the coast at Puri. This distinctive feature probably served as a navigational point for the European sailors during the maritime trade between Odisha, Bali, Java, and Sumatra.

The exact reason for the fall of the **DEULA**is still shrouded by controversy and the date of the collapse is also not certain. Several theories have indicated that eventually the crown stone was dismantled, broken or stolen which ultimately led to the collapse of **DEULA.**

According to one theory, the Konark temple is known to have suffered heavy damage in the year **1568 A.D**. by an invader, **Kala Pahad**of Bengal, the general of Karani Sultanate. The reference for the same is found in the **Madala Panji**of Puri Jagannath temple. The story goes on something like this. **Kalapahad**somehow knew the mechanics of the levitation of the idol. He destroyed the graphite blocks into pieces as a result of which the idol spiraled and hit the crown stone at **about 200 feet**above the base. Since he wanted the diamond, he shouted “Break the crown stone” and his men climbed the sanctum. They managed to displace the heavy crown stone and the deity collapsed with the rubble on the floor. It is said that **Kalapahad**pulled out the diamond with a burst of demonic laughter and defaced the remaining sculptors on the way to the exit. The displacement of the crown stone thus made a way for the **DEULA**to collapse sometime later.

Another age-old belief is that the magnetic pull of the crown stone was so strong that it made navigation very difficult for the sailors. It disturbed the functioning of ships’ compasses. Often, vessels passing through the Konark were drawn to it, resulting in the wreckage. Legends say that to save their shipping, the Portuguese voyagers took away the crown stone. Some say that it was taken by British Voyagers and that due to its displacement; the walls of the **DEULA**lost the balance and eventually fell down. But there is no historical record to prove the existence of such a powerful magnet at the Konark Temple.

There are still many other speculations regarding the fall of the **DEULA**. Some implicate the possible role of earthquake and thunderstruck. But such arguments have been refuted based on some substantial pieces of evidence. Let us now meet at the**DEULA.**

CHAPTER THREE

DEULA

The main sanctumor **DEULA** housed the deity of the Sun god. It has collapsed inward and only the ruins exist now. It is now without a roof and most of the original parts are no more. Behind these ruins is a platform with large mythical lion sculptors and a broken figure of hippopotamus which were probably a part of the sanctum's exterior.

The simhasana or the seat of the idol is still in existence within the ruins of **DEULA**. It is made of chlorite. A semicircular channel was also provided on the pedestal for easy flow of water from the body of the idol. Its base and sides are decorated with beaded borders, enclosing rows of elephants and various scenes from day-to-day life. The King and Queen can be seen sitting in front. The floor is also paved with chlorite slabs.

The entire temple complex was constructed by interlocking iron plates between every two stone pieces. The stones were originally polished in such a way that the joints were hardly visible. These iron plates are today visible in some parts of the temple due to weathering of the stones. You can keep an eye to catch the glimpse of such iron plates while moving around. It is thought that this entire metal skeleton was held together by a crown stone of the **DEULA**which was supposedly a massive 52000

Kilogram magnet! The statue of the Sun God inside the **DEULA**was probably made of astadhatu or an alloy of 8 metals. It makes sense because often one can see that the statues in Indian temples are made of astadhatus. Due to the unique arrangements of the reinforced magnets around the temple walls, the idol in the **DEULA**was able to float in midair, without any physical support. This theory has been widely acknowledged by the locals.

The placement of the **DEULA**and the Sun God had been aligned in such a way that at dawn, the first Sun rays from the coast would cross the **Jagamohana**through **NataMandira**and hit the diamond placed at the crown of the Sun God. This would light up the entire sanctum based on the principles of reflection and refraction! This dazzling display of light was at its best during Equinox.

It is said that the Pandas of Konark took away the idol out of the temple and hid it under sand for some years, during the invasion of **Kalapahad.**Some say that later on the idol was shifted to the temple of Indra, in the compound of the Puri Jagannath temple. Still, some say that the idol is yet to be discovered.

You can walk and climb up to the porch of the **Jagamohana** while screening through the visible artwork of the temple complex. At the same time let us narrate the history of the temple construction.

King Narasimhadeva I, of **"theEastern Ganga dynasty"**, who defended his empire against many attacks from Muslim rulers and have reigned from **1238 – 1264 A.D.** has been credited with the construction of this temple. It will be interesting to note that, **"the Ganga Dynasty"**is thought to carry out trade and exchange of knowledge with East Asia and African countries, especially Egypt.

According to historical records, very few in numbers though, this extraordinary structure was designed by the chief architect **Bishu Maharana**. He was an expert in **ferromagnetism**and took a special interest in ancient Egyptian structural engineering. The construction work was most probably initiated in the year **1243 A.D.**and completed in **1255 A.D.**with **1200**artisans, some say **12000**, and working tirelessly over an exhaustive period of **12 years**. This period is indeed very short given the representation of iconography on such a grand scale with every inch-space just so wonderfully carved.

Although the entire construction work of the temple was completed within the stipulated time, the final task of balancing the deity without a tilt in midair was lagging behind. The biggest challenge for the workers was the complex positioning of the diamagnetic substance or the graphite slabs that has a property of repelling the magnetic field and placing the 52-ton crown stone or Dadhinauti as the lifter magnet. Hence, the experts struggled a little too long than the stipulated time, not having any idea on how to complete the pending task.

Legend says that the king issued a final command to behead all the workers in case they failed to accomplish the task within a stipulated date. It was then that **Dharmapada**the **12**-year-old son of the chief architect **Bisu Maharana**arrived as a visiting onlooker. **Bisu Maharana**saw his son for the first time because he was away from home all this while. Both father and son had some moments of delight but soon **Dharmapada**became conscious of the impending danger to the lives of the workers. **Dharmapada**grew up playing with Bisu

Maharana's large collection of magnets back home since his childhood and exactly knew how to float a magnet. He executed the work flawlessly by sandwiching the graphite blocks with Bismuth and adjusting their positions. In few moments the deity was suspending impeccably at a balance in midair without a slight tilt.

However, the dilemma among the worker community now was that if the king gets to know that the task was accomplished by **1200 + 1**workers rather than **1200** then anyway he would kill them all. It is said that in the silence of the night **Dharmapada**sacrificed his life by jumping into the Chandrabhaga River from the top of the temple in order to save the lives of **1200 workers**. Soon the king was alarmed to know about the incident. There are different versions of this folklore though.

Since the temple became unholy with the death of **Dharmapada**, it is said that the Sun God was never worshipped there. But some believe that the regular worship of the deity was common till the eighteenth century. However, it can be rightly said that the one thing that makes the temple lively, is the spirit of **Dharmapada.**

CHAPTER FOUR

JAGA MOHANA

Enter Caption

The **Jagamohana**, the principal structure in the surviving ruins, is one of the grandest monuments of India. Even in this state, **Jagamohana**is still a wonder to the whole world. It is a live demonstration of collective human effort, limitless imagination, and great architectural craftsmanship.

This immense structure was carved from a rock so as to look like an enormous chariot of Sun god, moving towards the **eastern**direction, drawn by galloping horses. Originally the structure had seven horses. Four on the right and three on the left side. However, the sculptors of the horses are now in a disintegrated state. The whole structure gives an impression as if the chariot is ready to move. The structure will surely surprise anybody as it is a massive conception of artwork on stone-built without any modern tools. It is not possible to build another such monument with equal engineering brilliance.

The temple is now under restoration as a large part of it has been damaged over time. A huge part of the temple has turned to ruins and is still weathering away. The entrance door to the **Jaganmohan**a is currently closed due to the rapid fall of debris and stones from the ceiling. Entry inside the temple was banned in **1903**by the then Lieutenant governor of Bengal, J. A. Baurdilon. He ordered the temple to be sealed and filled with sand to prevent the collapse of the **Jagamohana**. In **1906**, casuarinas and punning trees were planted facing the sea to buffer the site against sand-laden winds.

The temple plan included all the traditional elements of a Hindu temple and is built of different types of stones, which are thought to be brought from the hills of Khandagiri and Udayagiri about 100 kilometers from Konark. Chlorite was used for the door lintel and frames as well as some sculptures. Laterite was used for the core of the platform and staircases near the foundation. Khondalite was used for other parts of the temple. None of these stones occur naturally nearby.

The porch of the **Jagamohana** consists of four main zones: the **platform**, the **wall**, the **trunk**, and the crowning head called **mastaka**. The first three are square while the **mastaka** is circular. The walls of the **Jagamohana** are 100 feet or 30 meters tall. The surviving structure has three tiers of six pidas each. These diminish incrementally and repeat the lower patterns. The pidas are divided into terraces. On each of these terraces stand statues of either dancers or musician figures.

A little ahead on the porch facing the **Nata Mandira,**You can figure out a horse like figure. It looks as if it is pulling the chariot. The seven horses are symbolic of the seven days of the week and the seven colours of the rainbow. The seven horses of the Sun god, have been named in Bhagawat Gita, as 'Gyatri', 'Usnika', 'Anustuv', 'Vrihati', 'Pangti', 'Tristup' and 'Jagati'.

According to historical texts, a **major pillar**dedicated to God Aruna, called the **ArunaStambha** or **Aruna's pillar**, used to stand in front of the eastern stairs of the porch between the **Jagamohana**and the **Nata Mandira**. This pillar is 10.26 meters tall and is intricately carved with horizontal friezes and motifs. However, during the troubled time, it was moved and placed at the lion's gate of the Jagannatha temple at Puri by a Maratha brahmachari known as Goswami.

You can walk up to most of the exterior for close-up views of exquisite stone sculptures with a wide variety of subjects. You will find sculptures in disintegrated as well as reasonable shapes which has many stories to say. The sad part is that most portions of the temples are in ruins especially the top parts where several sections have been replaced probably with plain stones to keep the structure standing.

In a way, the work of the artisans here is poetry in stone. The walls are adorned with intricate sculptures depicting life in every aspect. The details on the sculptures are truly amazing. There are thousands of images which include deities, celestial and human musicians; dancers, lovers, battles, hunts, animals and mythological creatures. The design of the temple is a mixture of abstract and geometry which are pleasing to the eyes and surprising to the mind. There is a very good chance that it was done for a valuable, scientific purpose because, in the ancient era, temples also served as a seat of higher education.

The intricate carvings in stone show the Way of life in three different stages - 1) Childhood, 2) Adulthood 3) Old Age. The lower portions depict animal and plant life, with humans and their community, family and social life forming the mid-section. Rishis or holy saints reside in the higher levels.

The walls are ornamented with carvings of Hindu deities and images from the daily life of the people, various animals, aquatic creatures, birds, mythological creatures, and friezes narrating the Hindu texts. These include Lord Vishnu's ten incarnations or Dasavatara, various kings of the Ganga Dynasty, several dancing girls, victory march, Naga mithunas or couples, individual naga figures, hunting scenes and so on. Some panels show images from the life of the king such as one showing him receiving counsel from a guru, where the artists symbolically portrayed the king as much smaller than the guru, with the king's sword resting on the ground next to him.

The moldings at the bottom of the platform contains friezes of elephants, marching soldiers, musicians, and images depicting the secular life of the people, including hunting scenes, a caravan of domesticated animals, people carrying supplies on their head or with the help of a bullock cart, travelers preparing a meal along the roadside, and festive processions. Girls are shown wringing their wet hair, standing by a tree, looking from a window, playing with pets, putting on makeup while looking into a mirror, playing musical instruments such as the vina, chasing away a monkey who is trying to snatch items, a family taking leave of their elderly grandmother who seems dressed for a pilgrimage, a mother blessing her son, a teacher with students, a yogi during a standing *asana*, a warrior being greeted with a namaste, a mother with her child, an old woman with a walking stick and a bowl in her hands, comical characters, among others. The platform at the base also has a sculpture of Lord Shiva as Nataraja.

The **Jagamohana**is also known for its erotic sculptures of **maithunas**or couples. It depicts Kamasutra as much as it depicts gods and goddesses. The themes show couples in various stages of courtship and intimacy and are also the second largest collection of erotic sculptures, after **Khajuraho**. Erotic sculptures are found especially in niches halfway up the porch, along the sides of the platform and around the doorways of the main building. These images are included with other aspects of human life as well as deities that are typically associated with tantratradition.

CHAPTER FIVE

WHEELS OF THE TEMPLE

The 24 giant wheels are beautifully carved. Each wheel has a diameter of about 10 feet or 3 meters with a lot of artwork around their axis and peripheries. The artwork of every wheel is different. Some of the wheels are intact today while some are not. These wheels are on the northern and southern sides of the temple complex. The replica of the same is available in stone, silver and wood. You may buy one in case you are enthusiastic about it.

These wheels are symbolic and represented too in some currency notes of Indian rupees. The 12 pairs of wheels represent the 12 months in a year or possibly the 12 zodiac signs, with each wheel in a pair representing Shukla and Krishna paksha of a month. According to others, the wheels of the chariot have been interpreted as the 'Wheel of Life' that portrays the cycle of creation, preservation and achievement of realization. Some also believe that it symbolizes "The Wheel of Karma" or "The Wheel of the Law".

The thicker ones are all carved with circular medallions at their centers on the widest part of the face. The axels of the wheels project by about one foot from the surface, having similar decorations at their ends. The rims are carved with designs of foliages with various birds and animals, whereas the medallions in the spokes are carved with the figures of women in various luxurious poses, mostly of erotic nature.

The architects knew solar geometry as well! The spokes of the wheels can create a sundial. One can calculate the exact time of the day by just looking at the shade cast by these spokes. Each wheel has 8 wider spokes and 8 thinner spokes. The 8 wider spokes divide 24 hours into 8 equal parts called prahars which is of 3 hours or 180 minutes duration each. Each minor spoke runs exactly in the middle of 2 major spokes. This means that the minor spoke divides the 3 hours in half, so the time between a major spoke and a minor spoke is an hour and a half or 90 minutes. The edge of the wheel has a lot of beads. There are 30 beads between one wider spoke to the next thinner spoke and each bead represents a value of 3 minutes. The Sundial shows time in anti-clockwise and the top center wider spoke represents 12 o'clock midnight. It is thought that out of the 24 wheels, 2 wheels show the time accurately from sunrise to sunset and the remaining 22 wheels can create moon dials too. However, nothing has been said with absolute certainty. Imagine the level of coordination between the astronomers, engineers and sculptors to create something like this.

CHAPTER SIX

PRESERVATION EFFORTS

The first suggestion to repair the ruin came from the unlikely direction of the Marine Board. In 1806 they submitted a proposal to have the temple repaired so that it could once more be a useful navigational landmark for the ships in the Bay of Bengal! But the government considered the expense involved being too great. This was again the reason given by the deputy governor of Bengal in 1838 when he refused to do anything to preserve the temple. In 1882-83, some jungle clearance was undertaken and a few statues mounted on platforms around the site, but in the wrong place. In 1892, Lieutenant Governor Sir Charles Elliot refused to grant any money for restoration, though some individual pieces of sculpture were shifted to the Calcutta Museum a couple of years later. Elliot did suggest that some debris be cleared from the rear of the porch, but this was not done, because the superintendent engineer thought that such action would weaken what remained of the building. Thus a hundred years were wasted before any constructive action was taken to improve the site. In 1900 Sir John Woodburn, the new lieutenant governor, visited Konark and immediately issued an order that repair and restoration should begin without further delay.

The Temple complex has ruins of many subsidiary shrines and monuments around the main temple. One can explore them one by one.

- **Bhoga Mandapa or the kitchen** – This monument was discovered in excavations in the 1950s. It includes means to bring water, cisterns to store water, drains, a cooking floor, and depressions on the floor probably for pounding spices or grains, as well as several triple ovens or chulahs for cooking. This structure may have been for festive occasions or a part of a community feeding hall. According to Thomas Donaldson, the kitchen complex may have been added a little later than the original temple. A well is located north of the kitchen, towards its eastern flank, was probably built to supply water to the community kitchen.
- **Mayadevi Temple** – Located west-southwest from the entrance of the main temple, it has been dated to the late 11th century, earlier than the main temple. It consists of a sanctuary and an open platform. It was discovered during excavations carried out between 1900 and 1910. Early theories assumed that it was dedicated to one of Surya's wife and thus named the Mayadevi Temple. However, later studies suggested that it was also a Surya temple, albeit an older one that was fused into the complex when the monumental temple was built. This temple also has numerous carvings and a square mandapa is overlain by a sapta-ratha. The sanctum of this Surya temple features a Nataraja. Other deities in the interior include a damaged Surya holding a lotus, along with Agni, Varuna, Vishnu, and Vayu.

- **Vaishnava Temple** – Located southwest of the so-called Mayadevi Temple, it was discovered during excavations in 1956. This discovery was significant because it confirmed that the Konark Sun Temple complex revered all the major Hindu traditions, and was not an exclusive worship place for the Saura cult as previously believed. This is a small temple with sculptures of Balarama, Varaha, and Vamana–Trivikrama in its sanctum, marking it as a Vaishnavite temple. These images are shown as wearing *dhoti* and a lot of jewelry. The sanctum's primary idol is missing, as are images from some niches in the temple. The site's significance as a place of Vaishnavism pilgrimage is attested to in Vaishnava texts.

CHAPTER SEVEN

War Horses of Konark Temple

There are two gorgeously carved war horses in front of the southern side of the Konark Temple. They are each about 10 feet long and 7 feet high. The sculpture depicts each of them with its massive strength and energy crushing down the warrior. This figure of warhorse of Konark has been accepted as the symbol of the State Government of Odisha.

Odisha Government Symbol

It will be fascinating to visit the museum which is very close to the temple! It is situated near yatrinivas Konark. It is maintained by the Archaeological Survey of India and houses fallen sculptures of the temple.

Konark is also known for its colourful festivals which are held to preserve the cultural heritage of Odisha.

CHAPTER EIGHT

CHANDRABHAGA MELA OR CHANDRABHAGA FESTIVAL

Chandrabhaga Mela is the most popular and a weeklong festival celebrated during the month of February. This festival is dedicated to the worship of the Sun God at Konark. Thousands of pilgrims flock to Konark every year to take a holy dip in the Chandrabhaga River and then circumambulates the shrine or **Jagamohan**to worship the Navagraha stone which originally was above the eastern portal and is now set up in a small shed outside the compound.

CHAPTER NINE

Konark Dance Festival

One can also experience the beauty of classical dance forms of India at the Konark Festival of Classical Dances held in Konark in the month of December. It is organized by the Culture Department, Government of Odisha. Eminent classical dancers and singers across the country participate to perform before the live audience in an open-air auditorium set on the backdrop of Konark Temple. The festival showcases the dance traditions like Bharatanatyam, Kathak, Kuchipudi, Sattriya, and Mohiniattam, among others with Odissi being common on all days. The festival has assumed a kind of distinctive significance and importance for the timely efforts it has made towards the revival, preservation and continuation of the unique temple dance tradition of Odisha.

Along with the dance festival, the tourism department hosts an international sand art festival on the Chandrabhaga Beach nearby. The sand art festival sees participation from both established and junior sculptors, a majority of them being girls. At the open-air auditorium, an Odia food festival and a stone carving workshop are also organized. The Tourism Department of Odisha organizes packaged tours to Konark and Puri during the dance festival.

www.ingramcontent.com/pod-product-compliance
Lightning Source LLC
LaVergne TN
LVHW020048010425
807359LV00013B/262

* 9 7 8 1 6 4 7 6 0 9 7 9 5 *